THE MAYAN CITIES

HISTORY BOOKS AGE 9-12

Children's History Books

The Mayans built cities all through their empire, across southern Mexico and much of Central America. What were these cities like? Let's find out!

Ruins of a Mayan City

MAYAN CITIES

The Mayan cities were the administration centers for the Mayan Empire. In many ways they were like the city-states of classical Greece: each city controlled the area around it and managed its own affairs, and sometimes acted like an independent kingdom instead of like part of an empire.

S ome of the cities were joined to each other by limestone roads called "sacbeob". Nobody knows whether the sacbeobs were used for everyday purposes like taking goods and food from one city to another, or were only for ritual processions, or for some other purpose.

Many of the cities were abandoned after the fall of the Mayan empire, and hundreds are still hidden in the jungle and rough land of the area.

For a long while historians thought these structures were worship centers where people gathered for special events, not cities where people lived, brought up their children, and bought and sold things like food and clothing.

With recent discoveries, it is clear that most, if not all, of these cities served large populations that lived both in the city and in the nearby countryside. Some of the cities had populations of as many as fifty thousand people!

Mayan cities tend to be more widely dispersed throughout the empire than, say, the cities of Mesopotamia (read about that area in the Middle East in Baby Professor books like Art, Religion and Life in Mesopotamia). The cities that were on trade routes, and were in areas that could provide enough food to support a growing workforce and the demands of the wealthy rulers, grew into local capitals and power centers.

Tenochtitlan

THE SHAPE OF A CITY

Other cultures, like the Aztecs, laid out their cities according to very regular plans (read about them in Baby Professor books like Aztec Technology and Art). While Mayan cities had a central open area with the most important building around it, they let the rest of the city grow in a more organic, informal way.

Guatemala City

Temples, palaces, and other buildings would be torn down and replaced with larger or better structures as the city developed. It is often hard now to figure out where the edges of a Mayan City were.

S tone walkways linked the central plaza and
palaces in the middle of the city with smaller
squares and plazas in residential areas. Everyone
could, and did, get to the central plaza for big
events, ceremonies, and celebrations.

Unlike medieval European cities, Mayan cities did not have defensive walls and fortifications. Toward the end of the empire some cities added walls made of earth and wood to try to defend themselves from attacking enemies.

Tikal, one of the greatest of the Mayan cities, had over 10,000 different buildings and other structures within six square miles. The buildings were as humble as family homes with thatched roofs, and as grand as huge stepped pyramids with temples on the flat area at the top of the pyramid. Tikal, in what is now Guatemala, had at its peak more than 60,000 residents. That makes its population density (number of people per square mile) much higher than that of most cities in the Americas or in Europe at the time.

Mayan Ruins, Tikal
Pyramid

Almost all of the great buildings were built from blocks of limestone. Limestone, when it is newly exposed to the air in a quarry, is soft enough that you can cut it and work it with stone tools. That was a good thing for the Mayans, who had no metal tools! Finished limestone gets harder once it is out of the quarry, and hardens into a durable building material.

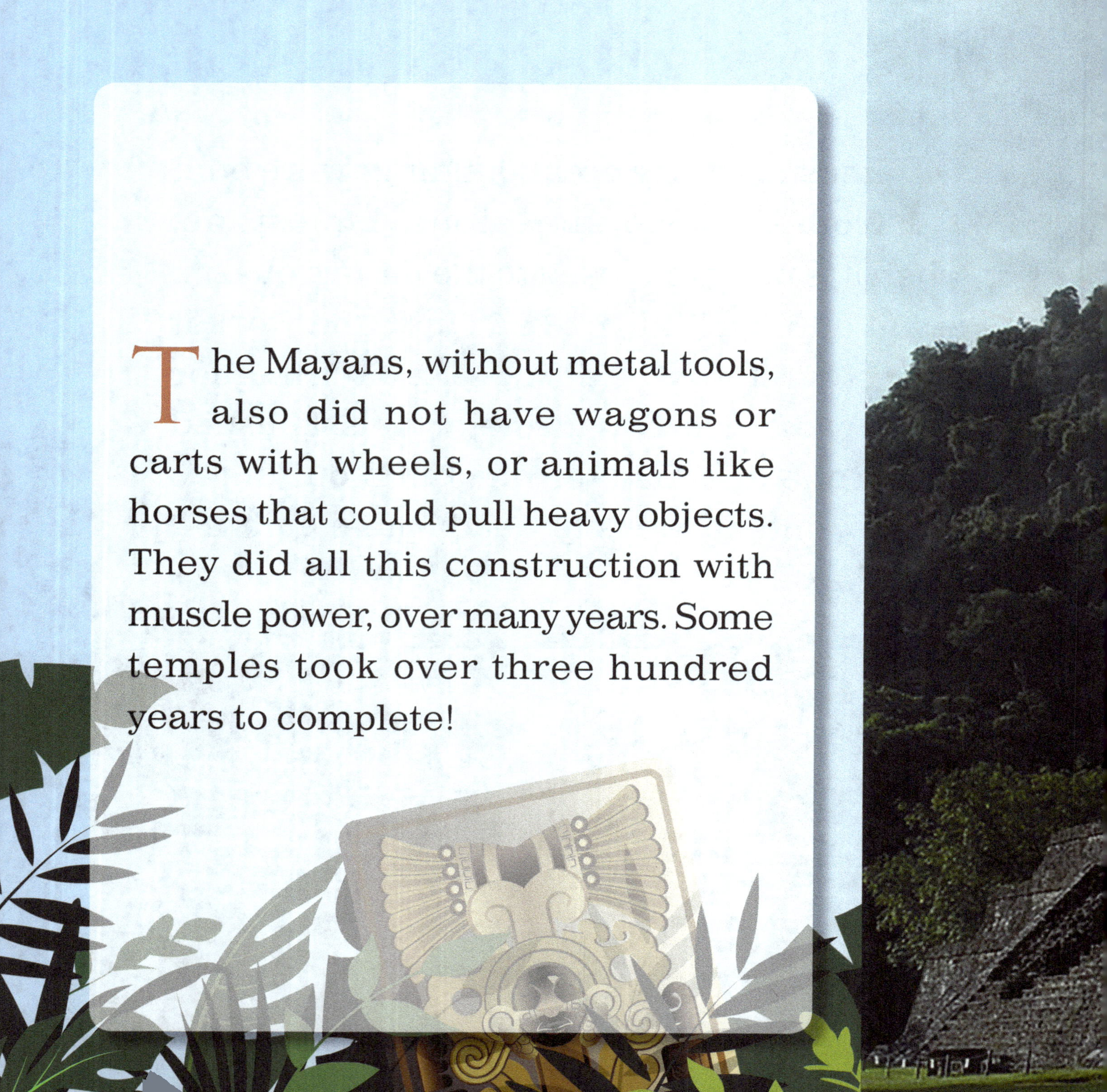

The Mayans, without metal tools, also did not have wagons or carts with wheels, or animals like horses that could pull heavy objects. They did all this construction with muscle power, over many years. Some temples took over three hundred years to complete!

The Mayans developed their city style and their taste in architecture over a thousand years, while their empire flourished. While many cities contain similar buildings and structures, most cities had their own style that reflected their local area and local resources.

THE MAIN BUILDINGS AND AREAS

The major Mayan cities had most of these elements, but some great cities were missing one or more of the building types:

PYRAMIDS

Egyptian pyramids have smooth sides that come together in a point at the top. Mayan stepped pyramids are like four giant staircases leading up to a flat top on which there may be a temple.

ome of them are up to two hundred feet tall. The pyramids and their temples were aligned in relation to the orbit of the moon around the Earth and the Earth's orbit around the sun. The Mayans used the temples for ritual ceremonies and human sacrifices.

The temples could have several rooms, but the rooms were very narrow, like passages. The main activities happened out on the flat top of the pyramid, where all who had gathered for the event could see what was taking place.

PALACES

Each royal family in the Mayan Empire lived in a palace located near the main temple of the city. These buildings were large and often complex, with many rooms. The palaces were on platforms like the temples at the top of pyramids, but the palaces were built much closer to the ground.

Mayan Governor's Palace

There could be courtyards, towers, roofed walkways, and fountains. Many workers and slaves probably also lived in each palace. There was also space for scribes, court and city officials, and other workers who kept the city and the empire functioning.

As the rooms in the existing palaces are small and not very comfortable, it is possible that the Mayan nobility also had more comfortable, informal residences, made of wood or similar material, that have not survived.

Interior of the House of the
Turtles in the archaeological
Uxmal enclosure in Yucatan,
Mexico

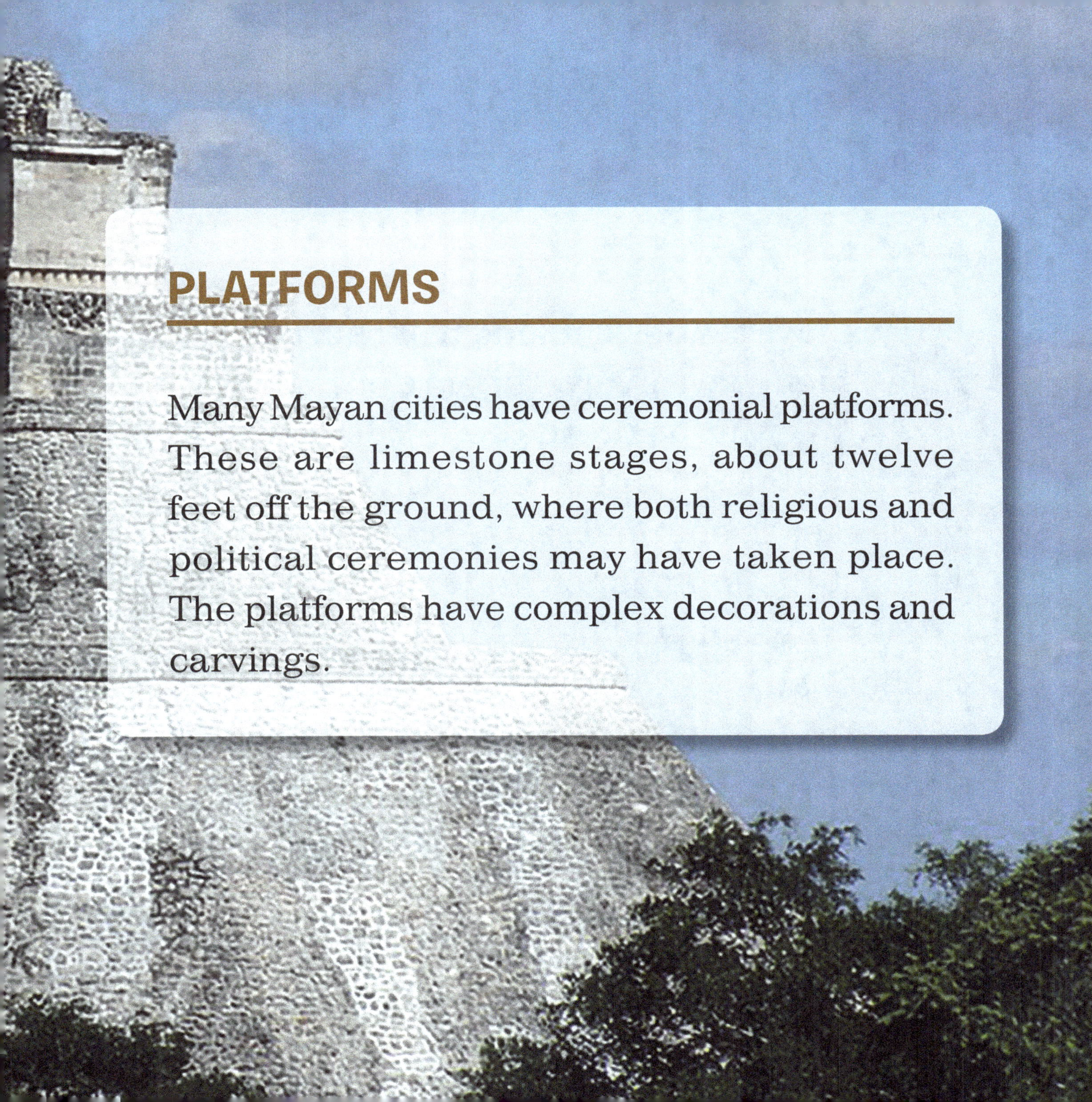

PLATFORMS

Many Mayan cities have ceremonial platforms. These are limestone stages, about twelve feet off the ground, where both religious and political ceremonies may have taken place. The platforms have complex decorations and carvings.

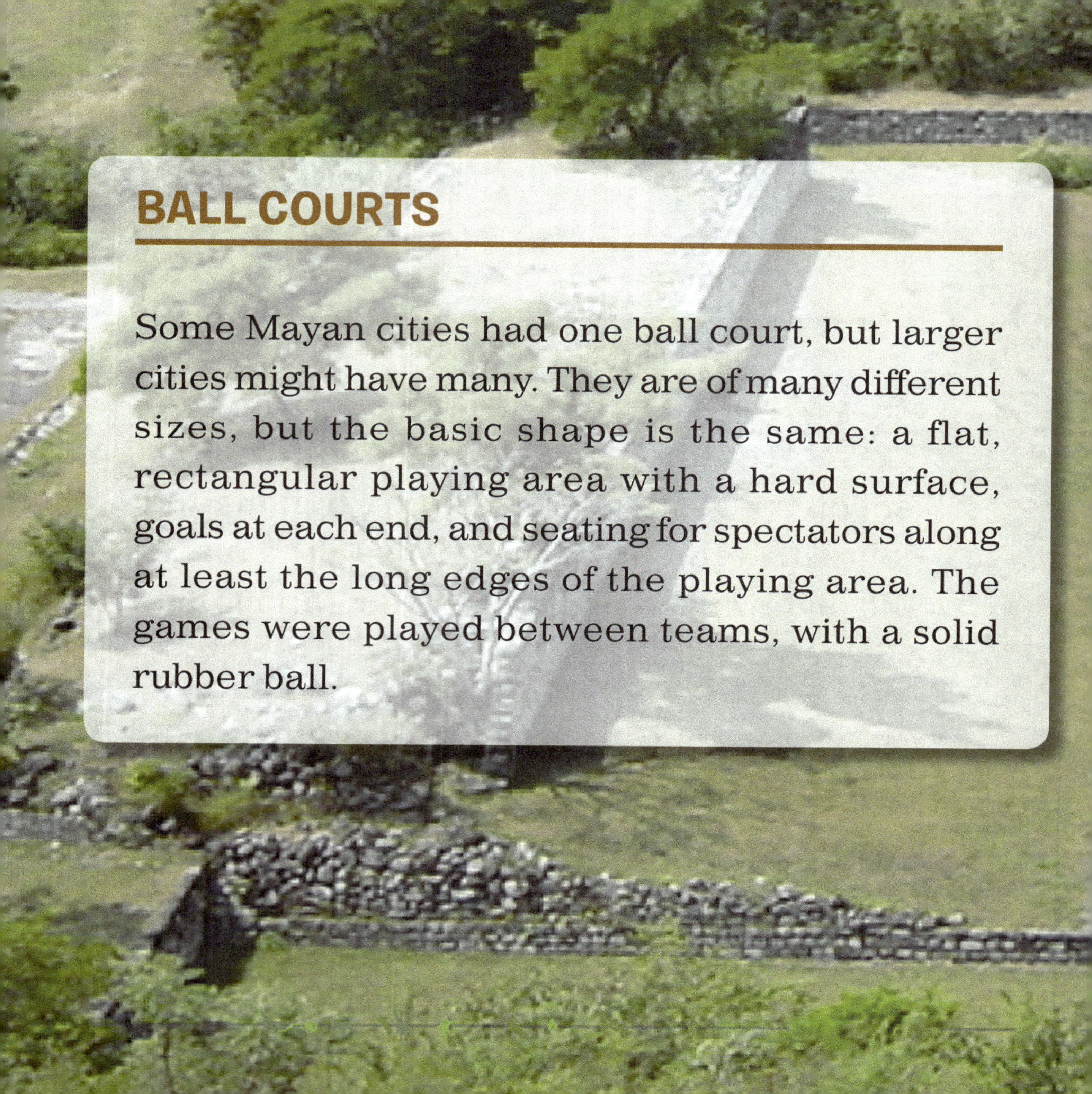

BALL COURTS

Some Mayan cities had one ball court, but larger cities might have many. They are of many different sizes, but the basic shape is the same: a flat, rectangular playing area with a hard surface, goals at each end, and seating for spectators along at least the long edges of the playing area. The games were played between teams, with a solid rubber ball.

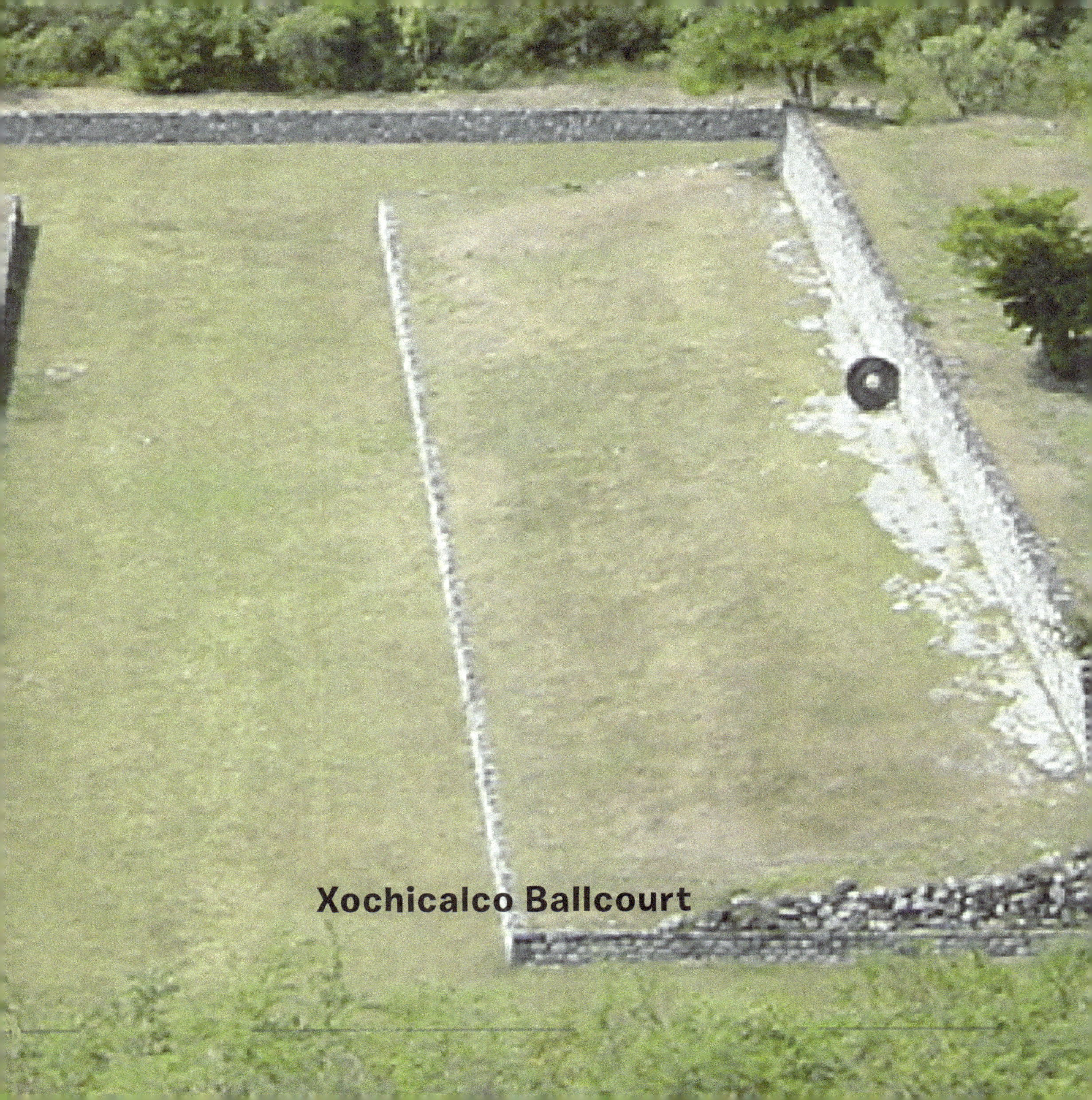
Xochicalco Ballcourt

Mayan Ball Players

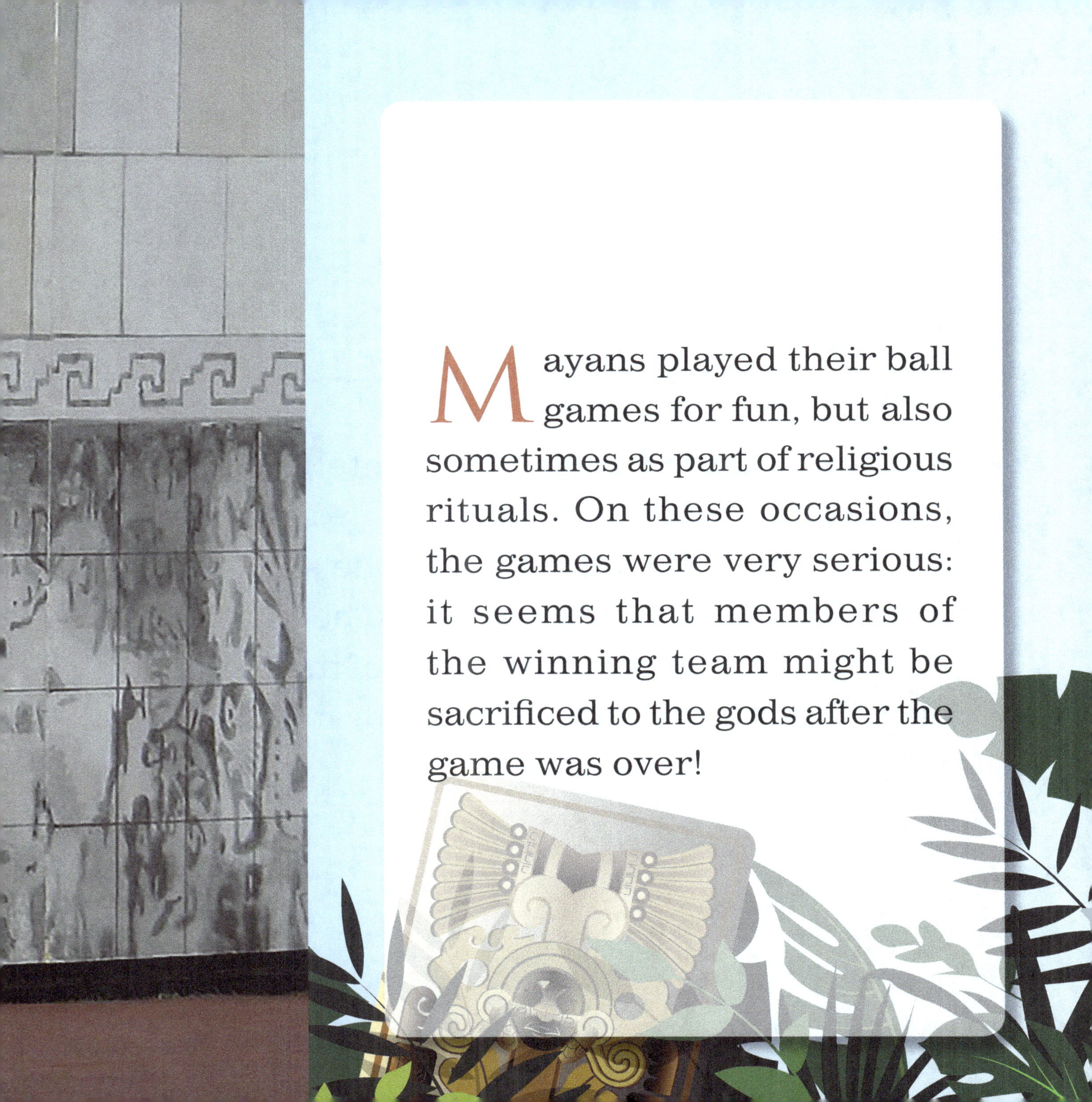

Mayans played their ball games for fun, but also sometimes as part of religious rituals. On these occasions, the games were very serious: it seems that members of the winning team might be sacrificed to the gods after the game was over!

STELAE

Stelae are carved pillars, elaborately decorated and describing the adventures of a great family or the victories of a king. Near the stelae there are often altars that would have been used for offerings to the gods in memory of the person or events that particular stela celebrated.

Monte Alban Stelae

RESERVOIRS

Where there was not a lot of water available, cities would have large reservoirs so everyone would have enough to drink in the dry season.

SWEAT BATHS

Some cities had buildings near important temples or palaces that worked like a sauna. You went into them and endured the high heat in the building created by a fire that slaves kept fueled. Probably the idea was that you could push bad thoughts, or bad spirits, out of your body along with the sweat.

Machu Picchu

RESIDENCES

People who did not rate palaces lived in buildings in residential areas further from the central plaza and the important temples. The buildings were built on platforms to raise them a bit above the ground, probably to protect against flooding in the rainy season.

BUILDING STYLES

Here are two distinctive elements of Mayan buildings:

THE ROOF COMB

The step pyramids that had a temple at the top often had a roof comb, a lattice-work of stone that rose higher above the flat area at the top of the pyramid and would have made the pyramid look even taller than it already was. The roof combs had no other function that we know of, but they were highly decorated with paintings and carvings.

THE MAYAN ARCH

European arches are curved, with a keystone at the top of the arch taking the inward pressure from both sides and keeping the arch from collapsing. Mayans favored a much narrower arch that produced an opening like a triangle. This probably relates to the Mayan belief that the underworld, the place of the dead, had nine levels.

All Mayan arches have nine pairs of stone blocks gradually drawing closer to each other until the top two blocks touch.

Adding a keystone would have added a tenth layer, which would have seemed wrong to the Mayan belief system.

THE MAYAN WORLD

There is much more to learn about the Mayans! Read Baby Professor books like *A Quick History of the Mayan Civilization*, *The Mayans' Calendars and Advanced Writing Systems*, *The Mayans Gave Us Their Art and Architecture*, and *The Daily Life of a Mayan Family*.

Visit
BABY PROFESSOR
EDUCATION KIDS
www.BabyProfessorBooks.com
to download Free Baby Professor eBooks
and view our catalog of new and exciting
Children's Books